The Black & White Puppy

A Story About the Biology of Love

By Miriam Grossman, MD
Illustrated by Laurel Dugan

The Center for Medical Integrity in Intimacy Education

Meet Jacob.

He lives with his mom, dad, and their dog Sophie.

Jacob loves doing puzzles, eating spicy foods like pickles and garlic, and going on adventures outside.

One night when Jacob was getting ready for bed, his dad came to the bathroom door.

"Jacob, come see! It's Sophie!"

"PUPPIES!" Jacob screamed with glee.
"And they're so tiny!"

Nestled close to Sophie were six newborns - three white, two brown, and one black and white.

"Why are they all squished together?" Jacob asked.

"They like it," Dad explained. "It's a special snuggle that lets them know they're loved."

Jacob was unsure. "Really?"

"Really - snuggling is like talking without words. It says *I love you.*"

Jacob grew excited.
"Can I hold the
black and white puppy?"

"No, not yet," Dad replied.

"Why not?"

"Because he belongs
with his mother now.
Her job is to keep him
warm and safe.
She won't let anyone
touch her babies,
not even their dad."

"Snuggling reminds the puppies of before they were born, when they were squished together inside Sophie, floating in a special kind of water."

"The water would taste
like the food she ate.
When you gave Sophie
peanut butter treats,
it would taste
like peanut butter!"

"That's funny!" Jacob said
scrunching his nose.

"So her puppies
will probably like
peanut butter too."

Suddenly, the black and white puppy climbed over his brothers and sisters to get some milk.

"Sophie's milk is perfect," Dad explained. "Not too hot or too cold. It even has vitamins."

"I like bear vitamins!" Jacob said.

"Nursing makes Sophie
happy and calm.
The more she does it,
the more she loves
her puppies."

"Dad, how does she know
how to take care of
her puppies?"

"While they were growing
inside her, Sophie was
changing. By the time the
puppies were born, she
knew everything moms
need to know, and
she was filled with love -
enough love for all six."

At this, Jacob began
to beg, "Can I hold the
black and white puppy,
pllllleeaasse?"

"Not now," Dad said, whispering. "He's fallen asleep and he needs to be with his mother."

"How come?"

"That's how he's made."

Jacob looked up at his dad. "When I have a bad dream, I like to sleep next to you and Mom."

"That's because we're also
made to be close," Dad said.
"The more we snuggle,
the more we love each other."

"Dad, now I know why I like spicy food!"

"You do?"

"It's because Mom ate spicy things while I was inside her!"

"You're exactly right. You were squished inside her for a long time."

"I bet I couldn't wait to get out." Jacob said.

"Actually, you loved it- just like the puppies."

"Would you like to know one big way puppies are different than people?"

"They have tails?" Jacob answered excitedly.

Dad laughed. "Yes. But also, puppies don't need their dad."

"Huh?" Jacob couldn't believe it.

"That's how we are different. Every child has a mommy and daddy, and needs both of them very much."

"Even before
you were born,
I loved you," Dad said,
reassuringly.
"That's why I sang
to you every night.
Even when you were
very tiny, smaller
than... a sprinkle on a
cupcake."

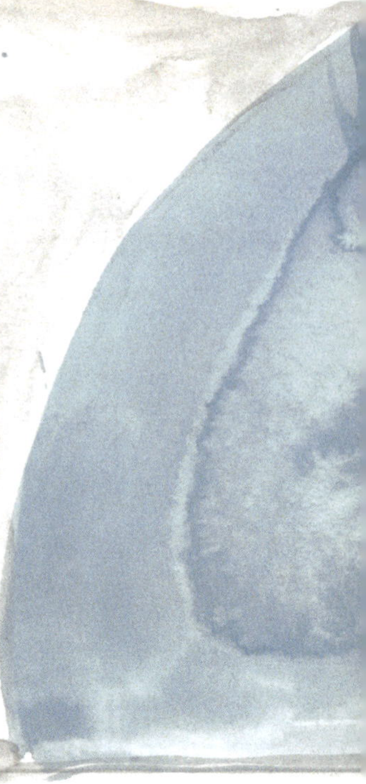

Jacob thought
about all he had learned:
how Sophie's puppies
floated inside her
all squished
together;

why he likes
the taste of
pickles and garlic;
and how snuggling
means *I love you*
without saying
the words.

Then Jacob's
mom called
from downstairs.
"Come pick out a book!
It's time for bed."

35.

Jacob snuggled close to his parents until he couldn't get any closer. His mom whispered in his ear, "When the black and white puppy is older, we want you to have him. Then you can hold him all you like."

They read his favorite
book together, and Jacob
felt warm and safe.
His parents' snuggle said
we love you
without words.

And very soon, just like
the black and white puppy,
he was fast asleep.

References

DeCasper AJ, et al (1980). Of human bonding: newborns prefer their mother's voices. *Science* 208:1174–1176.

Domínquez HD et al (1999). Interactions between perinatal and neonatal association learning defined by contiguous olfactory and tactile stimulation. *Neurobiol Learn Mem*. 71:272–288

Feldman, Ruth et al (2007) Evidence for a Neuroendocrinological Foundation of Human Affiliation. *Psychological Science* Vol 18 No.11 p965-970

Feldman, Ruth (2015) The Adaptive Human Parental Brain: Implications for Children's Social Development. *Trends in Neurosciences* Vol 38 No. 6

Herzog, James H (2009) Father Hunger and Narcissistic Deformation. Psychiatric Annals 39:3 156-163

Hepper P. (1988) Adaptive fetal learning: prenatal exposure to garlic affects postnatal preferences. *Anim Behav*. 36:935–936.

Hepper P (1995) Human fetal "olfactory" learning. *Int J Prenatal Perinatal Psychol.* 2:147–151.

Insel, Thomas R (1997) A Neurobiological Basis of Social Attachment. *Am J Psychiatry* 154:6 p726-735

Khaleque, Abdul et al (2012) Transnational Relations Between Perceived Parental Acceptance and Personality Dispositions of Children and Adults: A Meta-Analytic Review. *Personality and Social Psychology Review* 16(2) 103-115

Kinsley, C H (2006) The Maternal Brain. *Scientific American* Vol. 294 Issue 1, p72-79

Klaus, Marshall (1998) Mother and Infant: Early Emotional Ties. *Pediatrics* Vol 102 No.5 p1244-1246

Kosfeld, Michael et al (2005) Oxytocin Increases Trust in Humans. *Nature* Vol. 435 Issue 7042, p673-676

Mennella JA, et al (1995) Garlic ingestion by pregnant women alters the odor of amniotic fluid. *Chem Senses.* 1995;20:207–209

Rohner, Ronald (2001) The Importance of Father Love: History and Contemporary Evidence. *Review of General Psychology* Vol 5(4) p382-405

Schaal B, et al (2000) Human fetuses learn odors from their pregnant mother's diet. *Chem Senses.* 25:729–737

WHY I WROTE THIS BOOK

For the past ten years I've studied what children are taught about intimacy, gender, and family. As a child psychiatrist, I'm deeply concerned.

From Sydney to Seattle, Bogota to Toronto, children are told intimacy is about pleasure and condoms. They are led to believe that gender is fluid: *do you feel female today? Well, you're female then, because biology is irrelevant.* When it comes to family, children are taught only love matters – and anyone can love them. There's nothing special about their mothers and fathers.

These are dangerous falsehoods, and as a medical doctor I am worried about the systematic indoctrination taking place in classrooms all over the world. Yes, these are strong words. But the situation is ominous and warrants them.

When young people are taught to deny reality about fundamental aspects of life and indeed, of civilization, it endangers the individual child, as well as society as a whole.

Children must know the truth. First, that intimacy has emotional consequences. Science says touch is meaningful and creates feelings of trust and love. We are hard wired to attach.

Male and female are fixed conditions, at least for about 99.99 per cent of us. A man cannot become a woman, nor a woman a man.

Finally, every child has a mother and a father. If one of them is absent, due to tragedy or design, it creates a void. The child will have legitimate questions and feelings of loss. Especially unique is the bond between a mother and infant. It is filled with wonders!

"Children are like wet cement, whatever falls on them makes an impression." So warned the child psychologist Haim Ginott. Parents, you must be the first to make those impressions, and they must be deep. Empower your children with the biological facts found in *The Black & White Puppy* so they can reject, when they're older, the messages of activists who value social change more than truth.

I wrote this book because in order to make healthy decisions about love and family, people must be grounded in reality. In a better world, this project would not be needed. But this is the world in which we live.

Miriam Grossman MD

Special thanks to:

Beth Swift • Tanya Ofek • Chasida Halle
Greg Reese • Glorybell Daboub • Maribeth Harper
Laurel Dugan • Seamus Dugan • Molly Resnick
Elliot Resnick • Shmuel Pollen • Cristina Burelli

Other books by Dr. Grossman:

Unprotected:

A Campus Psychiatrist Reveals How Political Correctness in Her Profession Endangers Every Student

You're Teaching My Child WHAT?:

A Physician Exposes the Lies of Sex Ed and How They Harm Your Child

The Wonder of Becoming You:

How A Jewish Girl Grows Up

Please visit www.MiriamGrossmanMD.com and follow her at:

http://www.facebook.com/MiriamGrossmanMd

http://www.miriamgrossmanmd.com/blog/

http://twitter.com/Miriam_Grossman

ISBN 978-0-692-53661-2
www.MiriamGrossmanMD.com MiriamGrossmanMD@hotmail.com

85569072R00024

Made in the USA
Lexington, KY
02 April 2018